BOOK 3

CHRISTMAS HITS
for TEENS

8 GRADED SELECTIONS
FOR LATE INTERMEDIATE PIANISTS

ARRANGED BY DAN COATES

The *Christmas Hits for Teens* series presents carefully leveled, accessible arrangements for the teenage pianist. This series provides students with the fun opportunity to develop their technique and musicianship while performing their favorite Christmas songs and carols.

CONTENTS

Produced by
Alfred Music
P.O. Box 10003
Van Nuys, CA 91410-0003
alfred.com

Printed in USA.

ISBN-10: 1-4706-3886-X
ISBN-13: 978-1-4706-3886-3

THE FIRST NOEL

Traditional English Carol
Arr. Dan Coates

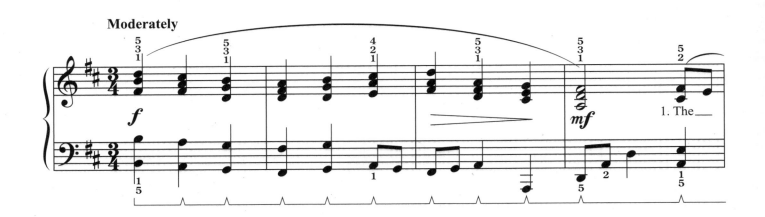

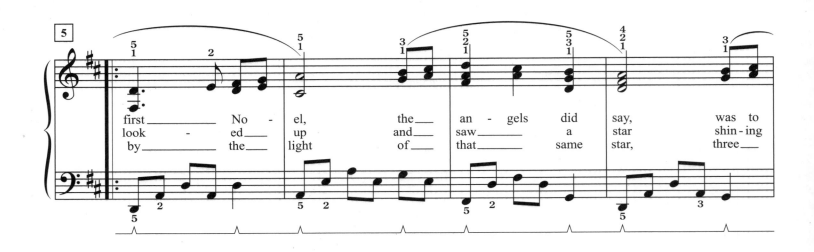

GOOD KING WENCESLAS

Words by John Mason Neale
Traditional
Arr. Dan Coates

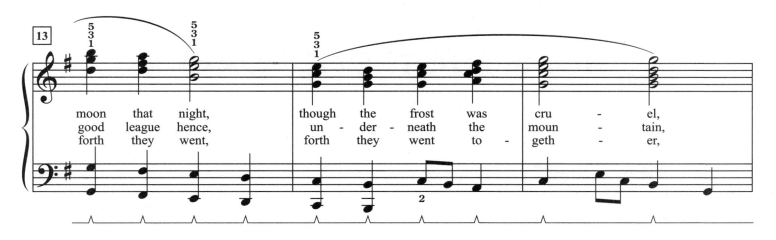

moon that night,
good league hence,
forth they went,

though the frost was
un - der - neath the
forth they went to -

cru - el,
moun - tain,
geth - er,

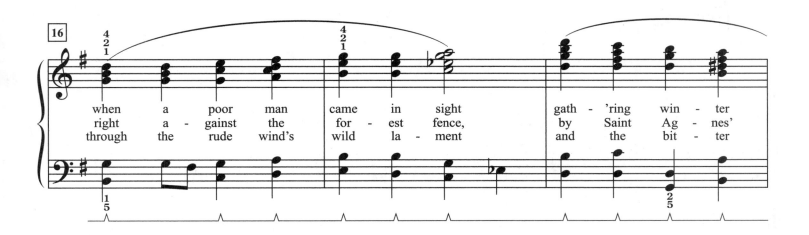

when a poor man
right a - gainst the
through the rude wind's

came in sight
for - est fence,
wild la - ment

gath - 'ring win - ter
by Saint Ag - nes'
and the bit - ter

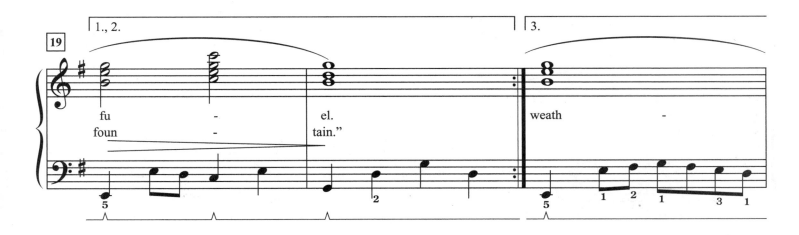

1., 2.

fu - el.
foun - tain."

3.

weath -

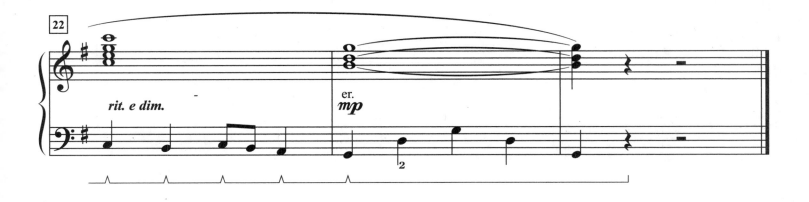

rit. e dim.

er.

mp

(THERE'S NO PLACE LIKE)
HOME FOR THE HOLIDAYS

Words by Al Stillman
Music by Robert Allen
Arr. Dan Coates

From Penn - syl - va - nia folks are trav - 'lin' down to

Dix - ie's sun - ny shore; from At - lan - tic to Pa -

cif - ic, gee, the traf - fic is ter - rif - ic. Oh, there's

no place like home for the hol - i - day, 'cause no

HAVE YOURSELF A MERRY LITTLE CHRISTMAS

Words and Music by
Hugh Martin and Ralph Blane
Arr. Dan Coates

I'LL BE HOME FOR CHRISTMAS

Words by Kim Gannon
Music by Walter Kent
Arr. Dan Coates

IT'S THE MOST WONDERFUL
TIME OF THE YEAR

Words and Music by
Eddie Pola and George Wyle
Arr. Dan Coates

"Be of good cheer."
friends come to call,

It's the
It's the

most
hap

won - der - ful
hap - i - est

time
sea

of the
son of

1.

year.

It's the

2.

all.

There'll be

UP ON THE HOUSETOP

Words and Music by Benjamin R. Hanby
Arr. Dan Coates

O HOLY NIGHT

Words by John S. Dwight
Music by Adolphe Adam
Arr. Dan Coates

Slowly, with reverence